Pet Sitting
Planner & Journal

Property of

_____

If found please contact

_____

MONTH OF:_____ Pet Sitting Type and time Block

Type of Service: 1- 24 hour in home, 2 – daily feed/ visit, 3 – daily feed/walk/ exercise

Mon	Tues	Wed	Thurs	Fri	Sat	SUN

Client Name	Contact Information

Client Name	Contact Information

WEEK OF: _____

Type of Service: 1- 24 hour in home, 2 – daily feed/ visit, 3 – daily feed/walk/ exercise

DAY	MON	TUES	WED	THURS	FRI	SAT	SUN

Pet and Service Details

Client Name _____ Phone _____

Dog _____ Cat _____   Pet Name   _____

Service Period From: _____   To:_____

Diet/food	Exercise Type	Medication

Vet Name _____   Contact Info_____ CLIENT NOTES AND

INSTRUCTIONS

Walking _____

Feeding _____

Exercise _____

Do's _____

Don't _____

Pet and Service Details

Client Name _____ Phone _____

Dog _____ Cat _____ Pet Name _____

Service Period From: _____ To:_____

Diet/food	Exercise Type	Medication

Vet Name _____ Contact Info_____ CLIENT NOTES AND

INSTRUCTIONS

Walking _____

Feeding _____

Exercise _____

Do's _____

Don't _____

Pet and Service Details

Client Name _____ Phone _____

Dog _____ Cat _____ Pet Name _____

Service Period From: _____ To:_____

Diet/food	Exercise Type	Medication

Vet Name _____ Contact Info_____ CLIENT NOTES AND

INSTRUCTIONS

Walking _____

Feeding _____

Exercise _____

Do's _____

Don't _____

Pet and Service Details

Client Name _____ Phone _____

Dog _____ Cat _____   Pet Name   _____

Service Period From: _____   To:_____

Diet/food	Exercise Type	Medication

Vet Name _____   Contact Info_____ CLIENT NOTES AND

INSTRUCTIONS

Walking _____

Feeding _____

Exercise _____

Do's _____

Don't _____

Pet and Service Details

Client Name _____ Phone _____

Dog _____ Cat _____   Pet Name _____

Service Period From: _____ To:_____

Diet/food	Exercise Type	Medication

Vet Name _____   Contact Info_____ CLIENT NOTES AND

INSTRUCTIONS

Walking _____

Feeding _____

Exercise _____

Do's _____

Don't _____

Pet and Service Details

Client Name _____ Phone _____

Dog _____ Cat _____ Pet Name _____

Service Period From: _____ To:_____

Diet/food	Exercise Type	Medication

Vet Name _____ Contact Info_____ CLIENT NOTES AND

INSTRUCTIONS

Walking _____

Feeding _____

Exercise _____

Do's _____

Don't _____

Pet and Service Details

Client Name _____ Phone _____

Dog _____ Cat _____ Pet Name _____

Service Period From: _____ To:_____

Diet/food	Exercise Type	Medication

Vet Name _____ Contact Info_____ CLIENT NOTES AND

INSTRUCTIONS

Walking _____

Feeding _____

Exercise _____

Do's _____

Don't _____

Pet and Service Details

Client Name _____ Phone _____

Dog _____ Cat _____   Pet Name   _____

Service Period From: _____   To:_____

Diet/food	Exercise Type	Medication

Vet Name _____   Contact Info_____ CLIENT NOTES AND

INSTRUCTIONS

Walking _____

Feeding _____

Exercise _____

Do's _____

Don't _____

Pet and Service Details

Client Name _____ Phone _____

Dog _____ Cat _____ Pet Name _____

Service Period From: _____ To:_____

Diet/food	Exercise Type	Medication

Vet Name _____ Contact Info_____ CLIENT NOTES AND

INSTRUCTIONS

Walking _____

Feeding _____

Exercise _____

Do's _____

Don't _____

TOOLS, TOYS, SUPPLIES NEEDED FOR TODAY

TOOLS	TOYS	SUPPLIES

CLIENT NOTES AND INSTRUCTIONS

_____

_____

_____

_____

_____

_____

_____

_____

DAY:

	CLIENT	PET
6 am		
7		
8		
9		
10		
11		
12 pm		
1		
2		
3		
4		
5		
6		
7		
8		

SPECIAL NEED PETS

_____
_____
_____
_____
_____
_____
_____

ACTIVITIES

_____
_____
_____
_____
_____
_____
_____
_____
_____
_____
_____
_____
_____
_____

VET INFO

_____
_____
_____
_____
_____
_____

TOOLS, TOYS, SUPPLIES NEEDED FOR TODAY

TOOLS	TOYS	SUPPLIES

CLIENT NOTES AND INSTRUCTIONS

_____

_____

_____

_____

_____

_____

_____

_____

DAY:

	CLIENT	PET
6 am		
7		
8		
9		
10		
11		
12 pm		
1		
2		
3		
4		
5		
6		
7		
8		

SPECIAL NEED PETS

_____
_____
_____
_____
_____
_____
_____

ACTIVITIES

_____
_____
_____
_____
_____
_____
_____
_____
_____
_____
_____
_____
_____

VET INFO

_____
_____
_____
_____
_____

TOOLS, TOYS, SUPPLIES NEEDED FOR TODAY

TOOLS	TOYS	SUPPLIES

CLIENT NOTES AND INSTRUCTIONS

_____

_____

_____

_____

_____

_____

_____

_____

DAY:

	CLIENT	PET
6 am		
7		
8		
9		
10		
11		
12 pm		
1		
2		
3		
4		
5		
6		
7		
8		

SPECIAL NEED PETS

ACTIVITIES

VET INFO

TOOLS, TOYS, SUPPLIES NEEDED FOR TODAY

TOOLS	TOYS	SUPPLIES

CLIENT NOTES AND INSTRUCTIONS

_____

_____

_____

_____

_____

_____

_____

DAY:

	CLIENT	PET
6 am		
7		
8		
9		
10		
11		
12 pm		
1		
2		
3		
4		
5		
6		
7		
8		

SPECIAL NEED PETS

_____

_____

_____

_____

_____

_____

ACTIVITIES

_____

_____

_____

_____

_____

_____

_____

_____

_____

_____

_____

_____

_____

_____

_____

VET INFO

_____

_____

_____

_____

_____

TOOLS, TOYS, SUPPLIES NEEDED FOR TODAY

TOOLS	TOYS	SUPPLIES

CLIENT NOTES AND INSTRUCTIONS

_____

_____

_____

_____

_____

_____

_____

_____

DAY:

	CLIENT	PET
6 am		
7		
8		
9		
10		
11		
12 pm		
1		
2		
3		
4		
5		
6		
7		
8		

SPECIAL NEED PETS

_____
_____
_____
_____
_____

ACTIVITIES

_____
_____
_____
_____
_____
_____
_____
_____
_____
_____
_____
_____

VET INFO

_____
_____
_____
_____

TOOLS, TOYS, SUPPLIES NEEDED FOR TODAY

TOOLS	TOYS	SUPPLIES

CLIENT NOTES AND INSTRUCTIONS

_____

_____

_____

_____

_____

_____

_____

_____

DAY:

	CLIENT	PET
6 am		
7		
8		
9		
10		
11		
12 pm		
1		
2		
3		
4		
5		
6		
7		
8		

SPECIAL NEED PETS

ACTIVITIES

VET INFO

TOOLS, TOYS, SUPPLIES NEEDED FOR TODAY

TOOLS	TOYS	SUPPLIES

CLIENT NOTES AND INSTRUCTIONS

_____

_____

_____

_____

_____

_____

_____

_____

DAY:

	CLIENT	PET
6 am		
7		
8		
9		
10		
11		
12 pm		
1		
2		
3		
4		
5		
6		
7		
8		

SPECIAL NEED PETS

ACTIVITIES

VET INFO

Client Name	Contact Information

Client Name	Contact Information

WEEK OF: _____

DAY	MON	TUES	WED	THURS	FRI	SAT	SUN

TOOLS, TOYS, SUPPLIES NEEDED FOR TODAY

TOOLS	TOYS	SUPPLIES

CLIENT NOTES AND INSTRUCTIONS

_____

_____

_____

_____

_____

_____

_____

DAY:

	CLIENT	PET
6 am		
7		
8		
9		
10		
11		
12 pm		
1		
2		
3		
4		
5		
6		
7		
8		

SPECIAL NEED PETS

_____
_____
_____
_____
_____
_____

ACTIVITIES

_____
_____
_____
_____
_____
_____
_____
_____
_____
_____
_____
_____
_____

VET INFO

_____
_____
_____
_____
_____

TOOLS, TOYS, SUPPLIES NEEDED FOR TODAY

TOOLS	TOYS	SUPPLIES

CLIENT NOTES AND INSTRUCTIONS

_____

_____

_____

_____

_____

_____

_____

DAY:

	CLIENT	PET
6 am		
7		
8		
9		
10		
11		
12 pm		
1		
2		
3		
4		
5		
6		
7		
8		

SPECIAL NEED PETS

_____
_____
_____
_____
_____
_____

ACTIVITIES

_____
_____
_____
_____
_____
_____
_____
_____
_____
_____
_____
_____
_____
_____
_____

VET INFO

_____
_____
_____
_____
_____

TOOLS, TOYS, SUPPLIES NEEDED FOR TODAY

TOOLS	TOYS	SUPPLIES

CLIENT NOTES AND INSTRUCTIONS

_____

_____

_____

_____

_____

_____

_____

DAY:

	CLIENT	PET
6 am		
7		
8		
9		
10		
11		
12 pm		
1		
2		
3		
4		
5		
6		
7		
8		

SPECIAL NEED PETS

ACTIVITIES

VET INFO

TOOLS, TOYS, SUPPLIES NEEDED FOR TODAY

TOOLS	TOYS	SUPPLIES

CLIENT NOTES AND INSTRUCTIONS

_____

_____

_____

_____

_____

_____

_____

_____

DAY:

	CLIENT	PET
6 am		
7		
8		
9		
10		
11		
12 pm		
1		
2		
3		
4		
5		
6		
7		
8		

SPECIAL NEED PETS

_____
_____
_____
_____
_____
_____

ACTIVITIES

_____
_____
_____
_____
_____
_____
_____
_____
_____
_____
_____
_____
_____

VET INFO

_____
_____
_____
_____
_____
_____

TOOLS, TOYS, SUPPLIES NEEDED FOR TODAY

TOOLS	TOYS	SUPPLIES

CLIENT NOTES AND INSTRUCTIONS

_____

_____

_____

_____

_____

_____

_____

DAY:

	CLIENT	PET
6 am		
7		
8		
9		
10		
11		
12 pm		
1		
2		
3		
4		
5		
6		
7		
8		

SPECIAL NEED PETS

ACTIVITIES

VET INFO

TOOLS, TOYS, SUPPLIES NEEDED FOR TODAY

TOOLS	TOYS	SUPPLIES

CLIENT NOTES AND INSTRUCTIONS

_____

_____

_____

_____

_____

_____

_____

DAY:

	CLIENT	PET
6 am		
7		
8		
9		
10		
11		
12 pm		
1		
2		
3		
4		
5		
6		
7		
8		

SPECIAL NEED PETS

ACTIVITIES

VET INFO

TOOLS, TOYS, SUPPLIES NEEDED FOR TODAY

TOOLS	TOYS	SUPPLIES

CLIENT NOTES AND INSTRUCTIONS

_____

_____

_____

_____

_____

_____

_____

DAY:

	CLIENT	PET
6 am		
7		
8		
9		
10		
11		
12 pm		
1		
2		
3		
4		
5		
6		
7		
8		

SPECIAL NEED PETS

ACTIVITIES

VET INFO

Client Name	Contact Information

WEEK OF: _____

DAY	MON	TUES	WED	THURS	FRI	SAT	SUN

TOOLS, TOYS, SUPPLIES NEEDED FOR TODAY

TOOLS	TOYS	SUPPLIES

CLIENT NOTES AND INSTRUCTIONS

_____

_____

_____

_____

_____

_____

_____

_____

DAY:

	CLIENT	PET
6 am		
7		
8		
9		
10		
11		
12 pm		
1		
2		
3		
4		
5		
6		
7		
8		

SPECIAL NEED PETS

ACTIVITIES

VET INFO

TOOLS, TOYS, SUPPLIES NEEDED FOR TODAY

TOOLS	TOYS	SUPPLIES

CLIENT NOTES AND INSTRUCTIONS

_____

_____

_____

_____

_____

_____

_____

DAY:

	CLIENT	PET
6 am		
7		
8		
9		
10		
11		
12 pm		
1		
2		
3		
4		
5		
6		
7		
8		

SPECIAL NEED PETS

_____
_____
_____
_____
_____
_____

ACTIVITIES

_____
_____
_____
_____
_____
_____
_____
_____
_____
_____
_____
_____

VET INFO

_____
_____
_____
_____
_____

TOOLS, TOYS, SUPPLIES NEEDED FOR TODAY

TOOLS	TOYS	SUPPLIES

CLIENT NOTES AND INSTRUCTIONS

_____

_____

_____

_____

_____

_____

_____

DAY:

	CLIENT	PET
6 am		
7		
8		
9		
10		
11		
12 pm		
1		
2		
3		
4		
5		
6		
7		
8		

SPECIAL NEED PETS

ACTIVITIES

VET INFO

TOOLS, TOYS, SUPPLIES NEEDED FOR TODAY

TOOLS	TOYS	SUPPLIES

CLIENT NOTES AND INSTRUCTIONS

_____

_____

_____

_____

_____

_____

_____

DAY:

	CLIENT	PET
6 am		
7		
8		
9		
10		
11		
12 pm		
1		
2		
3		
4		
5		
6		
7		
8		

SPECIAL NEED PETS

_____

_____

_____

_____

_____

_____

ACTIVITIES

_____

_____

_____

_____

_____

_____

_____

_____

_____

_____

_____

_____

_____

VET INFO

_____

_____

_____

_____

_____

TOOLS, TOYS, SUPPLIES NEEDED FOR TODAY

TOOLS	TOYS	SUPPLIES

CLIENT NOTES AND INSTRUCTIONS

_____

_____

_____

_____

_____

_____

_____

_____

DAY:

	CLIENT	PET
6 am		
7		
8		
9		
10		
11		
12 pm		
1		
2		
3		
4		
5		
6		
7		
8		

SPECIAL NEED PETS

ACTIVITIES

VET INFO

TOOLS, TOYS, SUPPLIES NEEDED FOR TODAY

TOOLS	TOYS	SUPPLIES

CLIENT NOTES AND INSTRUCTIONS

_____

_____

_____

_____

_____

_____

_____

DAY:

	CLIENT	PET
6 am		
7		
8		
9		
10		
11		
12 pm		
1		
2		
3		
4		
5		
6		
7		
8		

SPECIAL NEED PETS

_____
_____
_____
_____
_____
_____

ACTIVITIES

_____
_____
_____
_____
_____
_____
_____
_____
_____
_____
_____

VET INFO

_____
_____
_____
_____
_____

TOOLS, TOYS, SUPPLIES NEEDED FOR TODAY

TOOLS	TOYS	SUPPLIES

CLIENT NOTES AND INSTRUCTIONS

_____

_____

_____

_____

_____

_____

_____

DAY:

	CLIENT	PET
6 am		
7		
8		
9		
10		
11		
12 pm		
1		
2		
3		
4		
5		
6		
7		
8		

SPECIAL NEED PETS

_____
_____
_____
_____
_____
_____

ACTIVITIES

_____
_____
_____
_____
_____
_____
_____
_____
_____
_____
_____
_____
_____
_____
_____

VET INFO

_____
_____
_____
_____
_____
_____

Client Name	Contact Information

WEEK OF: _____

DAY	MON	TUES	WED	THURS	FRI	SAT	SUN

TOOLS, TOYS, SUPPLIES NEEDED FOR TODAY

TOOLS	TOYS	SUPPLIES

CLIENT NOTES AND INSTRUCTIONS

_____

_____

_____

_____

_____

_____

_____

DAY:

	CLIENT	PET
6 am		
7		
8		
9		
10		
11		
12 pm		
1		
2		
3		
4		
5		
6		
7		
8		

SPECIAL NEED PETS
_____
_____
_____
_____
_____
_____

ACTIVITIES
_____
_____
_____
_____
_____
_____
_____
_____
_____
_____
_____
_____

VET INFO
_____
_____
_____
_____
_____

TOOLS, TOYS, SUPPLIES NEEDED FOR TODAY

TOOLS	TOYS	SUPPLIES

CLIENT NOTES AND INSTRUCTIONS

_____

_____

_____

_____

_____

_____

_____

DAY:

	CLIENT	PET
6 am		
7		
8		
9		
10		
11		
12 pm		
1		
2		
3		
4		
5		
6		
7		
8		

SPECIAL NEED PETS

ACTIVITIES

VET INFO

TOOLS, TOYS, SUPPLIES NEEDED FOR TODAY

TOOLS	TOYS	SUPPLIES

CLIENT NOTES AND INSTRUCTIONS

_____

_____

_____

_____

_____

_____

_____

DAY:

	CLIENT	PET
6 am		
7		
8		
9		
10		
11		
12 pm		
1		
2		
3		
4		
5		
6		
7		
8		

SPECIAL NEED PETS

_____

_____

_____

_____

_____

_____

_____

ACTIVITIES

_____

_____

_____

_____

_____

_____

_____

_____

_____

_____

VET INFO

_____

_____

_____

_____

_____

TOOLS, TOYS, SUPPLIES NEEDED FOR TODAY

TOOLS	TOYS	SUPPLIES

CLIENT NOTES AND INSTRUCTIONS

_____

_____

_____

_____

_____

_____

_____

DAY:

	CLIENT	PET
6 am		
7		
8		
9		
10		
11		
12 pm		
1		
2		
3		
4		
5		
6		
7		
8		

SPECIAL NEED PETS

ACTIVITIES

VET INFO

TOOLS, TOYS, SUPPLIES NEEDED FOR TODAY

TOOLS	TOYS	SUPPLIES

CLIENT NOTES AND INSTRUCTIONS

_____

_____

_____

_____

_____

_____

_____

DAY:

	CLIENT	PET
6 am		
7		
8		
9		
10		
11		
12 pm		
1		
2		
3		
4		
5		
6		
7		
8		

SPECIAL NEED PETS

_____

_____

_____

_____

_____

ACTIVITIES

_____

_____

_____

_____

_____

_____

_____

_____

_____

_____

_____

_____

VET INFO

_____

_____

_____

_____

_____

TOOLS, TOYS, SUPPLIES NEEDED FOR TODAY

TOOLS	TOYS	SUPPLIES

CLIENT NOTES AND INSTRUCTIONS

_____

_____

_____

_____

_____

_____

_____

_____

DAY:

	CLIENT	PET
6 am		
7		
8		
9		
10		
11		
12 pm		
1		
2		
3		
4		
5		
6		
7		
8		

SPECIAL NEED PETS

_____
_____
_____
_____
_____
_____

ACTIVITIES

_____
_____
_____
_____
_____
_____
_____
_____
_____
_____
_____
_____

VET INFO

_____
_____
_____
_____
_____

TOOLS, TOYS, SUPPLIES NEEDED FOR TODAY

TOOLS	TOYS	SUPPLIES

CLIENT NOTES AND INSTRUCTIONS

_____

_____

_____

_____

_____

_____

_____

DAY:

	CLIENT	PET
6 am		
7		
8		
9		
10		
11		
12 pm		
1		
2		
3		
4		
5		
6		
7		
8		

SPECIAL NEED PETS

_____
_____
_____
_____
_____
_____

ACTIVITIES

_____
_____
_____
_____
_____
_____
_____
_____
_____
_____
_____
_____
_____

VET INFO

_____
_____
_____
_____
_____

MONTH OF:_____

Mon	Tues	Wed	Thurs	Fri	Sat	SUN

Client Name	Contact Information

WEEK OF: _____

DAY / CLIENT	MON	TUES	WED	THURS	FRI	SAT	SUN

TOOLS, TOYS, SUPPLIES NEEDED FOR TODAY

TOOLS	TOYS	SUPPLIES

CLIENT NOTES AND INSTRUCTIONS

_____

_____

_____

_____

_____

_____

_____

_____

DAY:

	CLIENT	PET
6 am		
7		
8		
9		
10		
11		
12 pm		
1		
2		
3		
4		
5		
6		
7		
8		

SPECIAL NEED PETS

_____
_____
_____
_____
_____
_____
_____

ACTIVITIES

_____
_____
_____
_____
_____
_____
_____

VET INFO

_____
_____
_____
_____
_____
_____
_____
_____

TOOLS, TOYS, SUPPLIES NEEDED FOR TODAY

TOOLS	TOYS	SUPPLIES

CLIENT NOTES AND INSTRUCTIONS

_____

_____

_____

_____

_____

_____

_____

_____

DAY:

	CLIENT	PET
6 am		
7		
8		
9		
10		
11		
12 pm		
1		
2		
3		
4		
5		
6		
7		
8		

SPECIAL NEED PETS

_____
_____
_____
_____
_____
_____
_____

ACTIVITIES

_____
_____
_____
_____
_____
_____
_____
_____
_____
_____
_____
_____
_____
_____

VET INFO

_____
_____
_____
_____
_____

TOOLS, TOYS, SUPPLIES NEEDED FOR TODAY

TOOLS	TOYS	SUPPLIES

CLIENT NOTES AND INSTRUCTIONS

_____

_____

_____

_____

_____

_____

_____

_____

DAY:

	CLIENT	PET
6 am		
7		
8		
9		
10		
11		
12 pm		
1		
2		
3		
4		
5		
6		
7		
8		

SPECIAL NEED PETS

_____
_____
_____
_____
_____
_____

ACTIVITIES

_____
_____
_____
_____
_____
_____
_____
_____
_____
_____
_____
_____
_____

VET INFO

_____
_____
_____
_____
_____

TOOLS, TOYS, SUPPLIES NEEDED FOR TODAY

TOOLS	TOYS	SUPPLIES

CLIENT NOTES AND INSTRUCTIONS

_____

_____

_____

_____

_____

_____

_____

_____

DAY:

	CLIENT	PET
6 am		
7		
8		
9		
10		
11		
12 pm		
1		
2		
3		
4		
5		
6		
7		
8		

SPECIAL NEED PETS

_____
_____
_____
_____
_____
_____

ACTIVITIES

_____
_____
_____
_____
_____
_____
_____
_____
_____
_____
_____
_____
_____
_____
_____
_____

VET INFO

_____
_____
_____
_____
_____

TOOLS, TOYS, SUPPLIES NEEDED FOR TODAY

TOOLS	TOYS	SUPPLIES

CLIENT NOTES AND INSTRUCTIONS

_____

_____

_____

_____

_____

_____

_____

_____

DAY:

	CLIENT	PET
6 am		
7		
8		
9		
10		
11		
12 pm		
1		
2		
3		
4		
5		
6		
7		
8		

SPECIAL NEED PETS

_____
_____
_____
_____
_____
_____

ACTIVITIES

_____
_____
_____
_____
_____
_____
_____
_____
_____
_____
_____
_____
_____
_____
_____

VET INFO

_____
_____
_____
_____
_____

TOOLS, TOYS, SUPPLIES NEEDED FOR TODAY

TOOLS	TOYS	SUPPLIES

CLIENT NOTES AND INSTRUCTIONS

_____

_____

_____

_____

_____

_____

_____

_____

DAY:

	CLIENT	PET
6 am		
7		
8		
9		
10		
11		
12 pm		
1		
2		
3		
4		
5		
6		
7		
8		

SPECIAL NEED PETS

_____
_____
_____
_____
_____
_____
_____

ACTIVITIES

_____
_____
_____
_____
_____
_____
_____
_____
_____
_____
_____
_____

VET INFO

_____
_____
_____
_____
_____

TOOLS, TOYS, SUPPLIES NEEDED FOR TODAY

TOOLS	TOYS	SUPPLIES

CLIENT NOTES AND INSTRUCTIONS

_____

_____

_____

_____

_____

_____

_____

_____

DAY:

	CLIENT	PET
6 am		
7		
8		
9		
10		
11		
12 pm		
1		
2		
3		
4		
5		
6		
7		
8		

SPECIAL NEED PETS

_____
_____
_____
_____
_____
_____

ACTIVITIES

_____
_____
_____
_____
_____
_____
_____
_____
_____
_____
_____
_____
_____
_____
_____

VET INFO

_____
_____
_____
_____
_____

Client Name	Contact Information

WEEK OF: _____

DAY / CLIENT	MON	TUES	WED	THURS	FRI	SAT	SUN

TOOLS, TOYS, SUPPLIES NEEDED FOR TODAY

TOOLS	TOYS	SUPPLIES

CLIENT NOTES AND INSTRUCTIONS

_____

_____

_____

_____

_____

_____

_____

_____

DAY:

	CLIENT	PET
6 am		
7		
8		
9		
10		
11		
12 pm		
1		
2		
3		
4		
5		
6		
7		
8		

SPECIAL NEED PETS

_____

_____

_____

_____

_____

_____

ACTIVITIES

_____

_____

_____

_____

_____

_____

_____

_____

_____

_____

_____

_____

_____

_____

VET INFO

_____

_____

_____

_____

_____

TOOLS, TOYS, SUPPLIES NEEDED FOR TODAY

TOOLS	TOYS	SUPPLIES

CLIENT NOTES AND INSTRUCTIONS

_____

_____

_____

_____

_____

_____

_____

_____

DAY:

	CLIENT	PET
6 am		
7		
8		
9		
10		
11		
12 pm		
1		
2		
3		
4		
5		
6		
7		
8		

SPECIAL NEED PETS

_____
_____
_____
_____
_____
_____

ACTIVITIES

_____
_____
_____
_____
_____
_____
_____
_____
_____
_____
_____
_____
_____
_____

VET INFO

_____
_____
_____
_____
_____

TOOLS, TOYS, SUPPLIES NEEDED FOR TODAY

TOOLS	TOYS	SUPPLIES

CLIENT NOTES AND INSTRUCTIONS

_____

_____

_____

_____

_____

_____

_____

_____

DAY:

	CLIENT	PET
6 am		
7		
8		
9		
10		
11		
12 pm		
1		
2		
3		
4		
5		
6		
7		
8		

SPECIAL NEED PETS

_____
_____
_____
_____
_____
_____

ACTIVITIES

_____
_____
_____
_____
_____
_____
_____
_____
_____
_____
_____

VET INFO

_____
_____
_____
_____
_____

TOOLS, TOYS, SUPPLIES NEEDED FOR TODAY

TOOLS	TOYS	SUPPLIES

CLIENT NOTES AND INSTRUCTIONS

_____

_____

_____

_____

_____

_____

_____

_____

DAY:

	CLIENT	PET
6 am		
7		
8		
9		
10		
11		
12 pm		
1		
2		
3		
4		
5		
6		
7		
8		

SPECIAL NEED PETS

_____
_____
_____
_____
_____
_____

ACTIVITIES

_____
_____
_____
_____
_____
_____
_____
_____
_____
_____
_____
_____
_____

VET INFO

_____
_____
_____
_____
_____

TOOLS, TOYS, SUPPLIES NEEDED FOR TODAY

TOOLS	TOYS	SUPPLIES

CLIENT NOTES AND INSTRUCTIONS

_____

_____

_____

_____

_____

_____

_____

_____

DAY:

	CLIENT	PET
6 am		
7		
8		
9		
10		
11		
12 pm		
1		
2		
3		
4		
5		
6		
7		
8		

SPECIAL NEED PETS

_____
_____
_____
_____
_____
_____

ACTIVITIES

_____
_____
_____
_____
_____
_____
_____
_____
_____
_____
_____
_____

VET INFO

_____
_____
_____
_____
_____

TOOLS, TOYS, SUPPLIES NEEDED FOR TODAY

TOOLS	TOYS	SUPPLIES

CLIENT NOTES AND INSTRUCTIONS

_____

_____

_____

_____

_____

_____

_____

_____

DAY:

	CLIENT	PET
6 am		
7		
8		
9		
10		
11		
12 pm		
1		
2		
3		
4		
5		
6		
7		
8		

SPECIAL NEED PETS

ACTIVITIES

VET INFO

TOOLS, TOYS, SUPPLIES NEEDED FOR TODAY

TOOLS	TOYS	SUPPLIES

CLIENT NOTES AND INSTRUCTIONS

_____

_____

_____

_____

_____

_____

_____

_____

DAY:

	CLIENT	PET
6 am		
7		
8		
9		
10		
11		
12 pm		
1		
2		
3		
4		
5		
6		
7		
8		

SPECIAL NEED PETS

_____
_____
_____
_____
_____
_____

ACTIVITIES

_____
_____
_____
_____
_____
_____
_____
_____
_____
_____
_____
_____

VET INFO

_____
_____
_____
_____
_____

Client Name	Contact Information

WEEK OF: _____

DAY / CLIENT	MON	TUES	WED	THURS	FRI	SAT	SUN

TOOLS, TOYS, SUPPLIES NEEDED FOR TODAY

TOOLS	TOYS	SUPPLIES

CLIENT NOTES AND INSTRUCTIONS

_____

_____

_____

_____

_____

_____

_____

_____

DAY:

	CLIENT	PET
6 am		
7		
8		
9		
10		
11		
12 pm		
1		
2		
3		
4		
5		
6		
7		
8		

SPECIAL NEED PETS

_____
_____
_____
_____
_____
_____
_____

ACTIVITIES

_____
_____
_____
_____
_____
_____
_____
_____
_____
_____
_____
_____
_____
_____

VET INFO

_____
_____
_____
_____
_____

TOOLS, TOYS, SUPPLIES NEEDED FOR TODAY

TOOLS	TOYS	SUPPLIES

CLIENT NOTES AND INSTRUCTIONS

_____

_____

_____

_____

_____

_____

_____

_____

DAY:

	CLIENT	PET
6 am		
7		
8		
9		
10		
11		
12 pm		
1		
2		
3		
4		
5		
6		
7		
8		

SPECIAL NEED PETS

_____
_____
_____
_____
_____
_____
_____

ACTIVITIES

_____
_____
_____
_____
_____
_____
_____
_____
_____
_____
_____
_____

VET INFO

_____
_____
_____
_____
_____

TOOLS, TOYS, SUPPLIES NEEDED FOR TODAY

TOOLS	TOYS	SUPPLIES

CLIENT NOTES AND INSTRUCTIONS

_____

_____

_____

_____

_____

_____

_____

_____

DAY:

	CLIENT	PET
6 am		
7		
8		
9		
10		
11		
12 pm		
1		
2		
3		
4		
5		
6		
7		
8		

SPECIAL NEED PETS

_____

_____

_____

_____

_____

_____

_____

ACTIVITIES

_____

_____

_____

_____

_____

_____

_____

_____

_____

_____

_____

_____

_____

VET INFO

_____

_____

_____

_____

_____

TOOLS, TOYS, SUPPLIES NEEDED FOR TODAY

TOOLS	TOYS	SUPPLIES

CLIENT NOTES AND INSTRUCTIONS

_____

_____

_____

_____

_____

_____

_____

_____

DAY:

	CLIENT	PET
6 am		
7		
8		
9		
10		
11		
12 pm		
1		
2		
3		
4		
5		
6		
7		
8		

SPECIAL NEED PETS

ACTIVITIES

VET INFO

TOOLS, TOYS, SUPPLIES NEEDED FOR TODAY

TOOLS	TOYS	SUPPLIES

CLIENT NOTES AND INSTRUCTIONS

_____

_____

_____

_____

_____

_____

_____

_____

DAY:

	CLIENT	PET
6 am		
7		
8		
9		
10		
11		
12 pm		
1		
2		
3		
4		
5		
6		
7		
8		

SPECIAL NEED PETS

_____
_____
_____
_____
_____
_____
_____

ACTIVITIES

_____
_____
_____
_____
_____
_____
_____
_____
_____
_____

VET INFO

_____
_____
_____
_____
_____

TOOLS, TOYS, SUPPLIES NEEDED FOR TODAY

TOOLS	TOYS	SUPPLIES

CLIENT NOTES AND INSTRUCTIONS

_____

_____

_____

_____

_____

_____

_____

_____

DAY:

	CLIENT	PET
6 am		
7		
8		
9		
10		
11		
12 pm		
1		
2		
3		
4		
5		
6		
7		
8		

SPECIAL NEED PETS

_____
_____
_____
_____
_____
_____

ACTIVITIES

_____
_____
_____
_____
_____
_____
_____
_____
_____
_____
_____
_____
_____

VET INFO

_____
_____
_____
_____
_____

TOOLS, TOYS, SUPPLIES NEEDED FOR TODAY

TOOLS	TOYS	SUPPLIES

CLIENT NOTES AND INSTRUCTIONS

_____

_____

_____

_____

_____

_____

_____

_____

DAY:

	CLIENT	PET
6 am		
7		
8		
9		
10		
11		
12 pm		
1		
2		
3		
4		
5		
6		
7		
8		

SPECIAL NEED PETS

_____
_____
_____
_____
_____
_____
_____

ACTIVITIES

_____
_____
_____
_____
_____
_____
_____
_____
_____
_____
_____
_____
_____
_____
_____
_____

VET INFO

_____
_____
_____
_____
_____

Client Name	Contact Information

WEEK OF: _____

DAY / CLIENT	MON	TUES	WED	THURS	FRI	SAT	SUN

TOOLS, TOYS, SUPPLIES NEEDED FOR TODAY

TOOLS	TOYS	SUPPLIES

CLIENT NOTES AND INSTRUCTIONS

_____

_____

_____

_____

_____

_____

_____

_____

DAY:

	CLIENT	PET
6 am		
7		
8		
9		
10		
11		
12 pm		
1		
2		
3		
4		
5		
6		
7		
8		

SPECIAL NEED PETS

_____
_____
_____
_____
_____
_____

ACTIVITIES

_____
_____
_____
_____
_____
_____
_____
_____
_____
_____
_____
_____
_____
_____

VET INFO

_____
_____
_____
_____
_____

TOOLS, TOYS, SUPPLIES NEEDED FOR TODAY

TOOLS	TOYS	SUPPLIES

CLIENT NOTES AND INSTRUCTIONS

_____

_____

_____

_____

_____

_____

_____

_____

DAY:

	CLIENT	PET
6 am		
7		
8		
9		
10		
11		
12 pm		
1		
2		
3		
4		
5		
6		
7		
8		

SPECIAL NEED PETS

_____

_____

_____

_____

_____

_____

ACTIVITIES

_____

_____

_____

_____

_____

_____

_____

_____

_____

_____

_____

_____

VET INFO

_____

_____

_____

_____

_____

TOOLS, TOYS, SUPPLIES NEEDED FOR TODAY

TOOLS	TOYS	SUPPLIES

CLIENT NOTES AND INSTRUCTIONS

_____

_____

_____

_____

_____

_____

_____

_____

DAY:

	CLIENT	PET
6 am		
7		
8		
9		
10		
11		
12 pm		
1		
2		
3		
4		
5		
6		
7		
8		

SPECIAL NEED PETS

_____
_____
_____
_____
_____
_____

ACTIVITIES

_____
_____
_____
_____
_____
_____
_____
_____

VET INFO

_____
_____
_____
_____
_____
_____

_____
_____
_____
_____

TOOLS, TOYS, SUPPLIES NEEDED FOR TODAY

TOOLS	TOYS	SUPPLIES

CLIENT NOTES AND INSTRUCTIONS

_____

_____

_____

_____

_____

_____

_____

_____

DAY:

	CLIENT	PET
6 am		
7		
8		
9		
10		
11		
12 pm		
1		
2		
3		
4		
5		
6		
7		
8		

SPECIAL NEED PETS

_____
_____
_____
_____
_____
_____
_____

ACTIVITIES

_____
_____
_____
_____
_____
_____
_____
_____
_____

VET INFO

_____
_____
_____
_____
_____

_____
_____
_____
_____

TOOLS, TOYS, SUPPLIES NEEDED FOR TODAY

TOOLS	TOYS	SUPPLIES

CLIENT NOTES AND INSTRUCTIONS

_____

_____

_____

_____

_____

_____

_____

_____

DAY:

	CLIENT	PET
6 am		
7		
8		
9		
10		
11		
12 pm		
1		
2		
3		
4		
5		
6		
7		
8		

SPECIAL NEED PETS

_____
_____
_____
_____
_____
_____
_____

ACTIVITIES

_____
_____
_____
_____
_____
_____
_____
_____
_____
_____
_____
_____
_____
_____
_____

VET INFO

_____
_____
_____
_____
_____

TOOLS, TOYS, SUPPLIES NEEDED FOR TODAY

TOOLS	TOYS	SUPPLIES

CLIENT NOTES AND INSTRUCTIONS

_____

_____

_____

_____

_____

_____

_____

_____

DAY:

	CLIENT	PET
6 am		
7		
8		
9		
10		
11		
12 pm		
1		
2		
3		
4		
5		
6		
7		
8		

SPECIAL NEED PETS

_____
_____
_____
_____
_____
_____

ACTIVITIES

_____
_____
_____
_____
_____
_____
_____
_____
_____
_____
_____
_____
_____
_____

VET INFO

_____
_____
_____
_____
_____

TOOLS, TOYS, SUPPLIES NEEDED FOR TODAY

TOOLS	TOYS	SUPPLIES

CLIENT NOTES AND INSTRUCTIONS

_____

_____

_____

_____

_____

_____

_____

_____

DAY:

	CLIENT	PET
6 am		
7		
8		
9		
10		
11		
12 pm		
1		
2		
3		
4		
5		
6		
7		
8		

SPECIAL NEED PETS

_____

_____

_____

_____

_____

_____

ACTIVITIES

_____

_____

_____

_____

_____

_____

_____

_____

_____

_____

_____

_____

_____

_____

_____

VET INFO

_____

_____

_____

_____

_____